ISBN 0-87666-981-X

Risa Teitler with the lutino
cockatiel she used as the
model for many of the
photographs in this book.
Taking an untamed, un-
trained bird, she had it
walking on her hands
within 15 minutes!

Distributed in the U.S. by T.F.H. Publications, Inc., 211 West Sylvania Avenue,
P.O. Box 427, Neptune, N.J. 07753; in England by T.F.H. (Gt. Britain) Ltd., 13
Nutley Lane, Reigate, Surrey; in Canada to the book store and library trade by
Beaverbooks, 953 Dillingham Road, Pickering, Ontario L1W 1Z7, Canada; in
Canada to the pet trade by Rolf C. Hagen Ltd., 3225 Sartelon Street, Montreal
382, Quebec; in Southeast Asia by Y.W. Ong, 9 Lorong 36 Geylang, Singapore
14; in Australia and the South Pacific by Pet Imports Pty. Ltd., P.O. Box 149,
Brookvale 2100, N.S.W., Australia; in South Africa by Valiant Publishers (Pty.)
Ltd., P.O. Box 78236, Sandton City, 2146, South Africa. Published by T.F.H.
Publications, Inc., Ltd., The British Crown Colony of Hong Kong.

TAMING AND TRAINING
COCKATIELS

by **Risa Teitler**
**PROFESSIONAL TRAINER,
PARROT JUNGLE,
MIAMI, FLORIDA**

An adult male cockatiel in full color.

Preface

This book is intended as a manual for the inexperienced bird owner. The information is not meant to be taken as the last word on cockatiel taming, nutrition and breeding; it is, however, the result of many years of professional experience in breeding and handling these birds. If you follow the information and develop a **training and feeding schedule**, you will undoubtedly enjoy owning a healthy, happy cockatiel.

Cockatiels are one of the most easily tamed caged birds. They fit well into the lifestyles of most people. Remember that you can learn the most about taming a bird by doing it yourself, but read the material given here and whatever else you can find on the subject. Additional books are listed in the bibliography at the back of this book. Talk to experienced people and those who own cockatiels. Use your common sense and don't accept unqualifiedly any advice that contradicts your own judgment.

Congratulations on acquiring your first, or possibly one of many, cockatiels, and please remember that you can't train a sick cockatiel, so pay attention to the following pages.

Risa Teitler

Cockatiels are one of the most easily tamed caged birds.

7

The bird should be tamed initially by the person most suited for the task.

Part of taming and training depends upon a suitable uncaged perch being available.

I
Introduction

Cockatiels, sometimes called *quarrion birds* in their native Australia, are steadily gaining popularity as caged birds. They are called "Cockies" by many professionals. Their availability, relative low cost, affectionate personalities and talent for mimicry recommend them as family pets.

In the wild state, cockatiels are found throughout the Australian sub-continent, traveling in pairs or small flocks. They feed on seedling grasses, fruits, berries, grains and to the dismay of farmers on cultivated crops. Migration of the birds is apparently linked to the supply of fresh water. Breeding generally occurs between August and September (Australian winter) but may vary considerably according to climatic changes.

Cockatiels are bred in several distinct color varieties. There seems to be little difference in their worthiness as pets, and the difference in cost is merely the rarity of the color. A normally colored cockatiel is shown on the facing page.

Approximately twelve inches long from graceful crest to slender tail, their plumage is predominantly grey, with a wide band of white on the wing. Mature males display a bright yellow head with orange patches over the ears. The upper side of the tail

Cockatiels, bred in South Africa, awaiting sale in Florida after having been quarantined. Photo at Gators of Miami.

is pearl grey, the underside is black. Immatures and females are distinguished by the yellow and black banding on the underside of the tail with facial yellow restricted to outlining the features. Young males begin to show color changes by six months of age. Once the first yellow feathers appear on the face, the entire head rapidly goes yellow.

Cockies are hardy birds with a life expectancy of 20 to 25 years. Aviculturists have produced some new varieties in addition to the normal grey bird described above. These include the lutino or white cockatiel first established as a reliable strain by Mrs. E.L. Moon, the pied, a beautiful bird with irregular patterns of white, grey and yellow all over the body, the pearly, cinnamon, and the silver cockatiel. More color mutations are appearing regularly, but like the colors of dogs, some are not interesting.

Gators of Miami, one of the largest importers and wholesalers of birds, houses their cockatiels in several different types of cage.

The wood is protected by screening lining the inside.

This is an easy-to-clean cage, since the droppings fall outside through the cage floor.

Long rows of large flights like this may also be used for breeding.

A lutino, or white, cockatiel. This is just one of the various mutants for which inbred strains have been developed. The cinnamons, on the facing page, are a relatively recent introduction. Photos by Harry V. Lacey and George Smith.

Once you have decided that a cockatiel is the bird for you, go to a few local pet dealers and see what they have to offer. Chances are you'll find the right bird at a reasonable cost. Now evaluate your ability as a trainer. Are you patient, calm and determined to win the friendship of your new bird? If you fit this description, you are almost assured of success. Cockatiels are ideal first birds for the young fancier, man or woman, who desires an amiable companion that requires a minimum of space and a simple diet. It is not a pet for young, irresponsible children to abuse.

Only one person should deal with the bird initially in the taming situation. Choose the most motivated family member with the greatest amount of time to devote to taming the bird. Once the bird is hand tame the other household members should endeavor to establish their own relationships with the cockatiel or he may develop into a one man bird.

Decide on a suitable location for the cage. Keep it out of the kitchen, where temperature may fluctuate and away from windows and other drafty spots. Placement near the door also subjects the bird to drafts, and if he flies the danger of escape is obvious. In cold climates, avoid housing the bird near radiators or heaters, since the dry heat may be detrimental. Some bird owners devote an entire room to their pets and if this is the case, the room can be designed especially for birds. Others allow their pets to fly free in a screened patio area, but care must be taken to bring them indoors in cold or rainy weather.

Outdoor aviaries for cockatiels are fine if adequate shelter from the elements is provided. The outdoor situation presents special problems for the bird owner in the form of neighborhood cats and dogs, and rodents that may eat the food provided for the birds. In addition, more attention must be given to keeping the birds free of pests such as feather mites and lice, which are rarely present on a caged house pet.

Outside, free flying for the cockatiel should be considered only if you are located far from busy streets and have enough property that no other residences are within sight or sound. Establish a definite feeding station and time and, as an added draw, you may want to acquire a second cockatiel to keep caged in full sight of the free bird. First, introduce the yard to a clipped bird. Give him every opportunity to familiarize himself with the surroundings. By the time his flight feathers have been replaced, he should consider himself part owner of the property and will have little inclination to leave. Again, a feeding area with plenty of fresh water and a regular feeding schedule will help train a free flyer to remain close to home. Don't expect to establish a free flyer in a short time. The whole process may take from a few months to a year. For most people, in fact, it is not a good idea at all to try to establish cockatiels as free flyers; there are too many dangers.

Choosing The Bird

Many people feel that it is necessary to buy two cockatiels, because one bird will be lonely. On the contrary, if what you want is a tame pet bird you should buy only one. A single bird is more easily tamed and taught to talk.

Now that you've decided on one bird or two, look for a pet dealer that has a clean shop, clean cages and feeders, and *employees that are able to answer your questions satisfactorily.* Availability of good quality feed and supplies, including cages, stands, toys and books may be other factors that influence your choice of a pet shop.

Don't buy your cockatiel from any department store where the person selling you the bird knows nothing about handling it. If they can't handle it, they probably couldn't care for it either.

The best candidate for an easily tamed pet is a young bird between 10 and 16 weeks of age. Obviously, a cockatiel that already shows a bright yellow head is at least six months old, and although it is possible to make a fine pet out of an older bird, it is much more difficult and time consuming. The purchase of a colored out (mature) bird has one advantage: there can be no mistake about the sex of the bird. Both males and females make good pets and can acquire speech, but the male cockatiel is usually a better talker.

If you are lucky enough to find a pet dealer that offers hand reared young, take advantage of the situation, for the bird will be tame when you get it. Otherwise make your choice on the basis of the following criteria.

Buy a healthy bird. Judge his health by observing how active he is at the pet shop. Stand back from the cage to avoid inhibiting the birds' natural behavior. The sassy birds that hop

A closeup of the head of a healthy immature female. Note the full crest, the clear eye and the clean nostrils.

When you select the bird that you want, look for an alert, inquisitive appearance.

from perch to perch, whistling, always trying to boss the other birds around, are most likely males.

The **plumage** must be smooth and no bare spots should be visible with the exception of the crown. The crown is devoid of feathers in all cockatiels, but in older birds is covered by surrounding plumage.

Eyes must be clear and bright, free of any discharge or swelling.

Nasal openings must not be clogged or runny.

Study the **droppings** on the cage bottom. They are the best indicators of health. Droppings should have good form, both dark green and white matter. Loose, watery droppings bright green in color indicate the presence of a digestive disorder.

Respiration should be slow and even, not labored or irregular.

Once you see a bird you like, examine him further when the pet shop employee removes him from the cage. Plan what you're going to look at to avoid restraining the bird any longer than necessary.

Does he have all his toes and claws? A missing toe or claw is no serious disability for the bird as long as no fresh wound or swelling is visible.

Feel the **bird's chest** to determine that he has good weight. A bird should be rejected if his breast bone protrudes sharply, indicating lack of weight and possible illness. Be sure to check the **vent** for any sign of soiling; a soiled bird should be rejected. **Check the wings** for lumps at the base of feathers. Make sure there are **no sores or wounds** anywhere on the body.

Any bird that sits fluffed up with his eyes closed or swollen, with discharge from the nostrils or soiled vent, should not be purchased, no matter how anxious you are to obtain a pet.

FOOD, FEEDING AND CLEANING

For optimum benefit to your bird, a standard maintenance diet is best kept simple and balanced.

Each day provide fresh sunflower seed, millet, oats, whole seed, parakeet or budgerigar seed, water with a commercially prepared vitamin supplement, and a portion of some green leafy vegetable such as wild lettuce, romaine, chicory, turnip tops, escarole, spinach, or carrot tops. They add important minerals and vitamins to the diet. Don't bother with iceberg (soft-leaf lettuce). It has no food value. Wash the raw leaves and place them in the cage. If given regularly, green leafy vegetables will not cause diarrhea.

You may want to take some bird seed and sprout your own seedling grasses, which will be greatly appreciated by your pet and eaten with relish. If the seed you offer your birds does not sprout, it is not good food.

Other fruits and vegetables that can be given are corn, peas, apple, orange, banana or just about anything that he enjoys.

Keep in mind that your cockatiel may not accept fruits and vegetables immediately. It may seem that he never takes a nibble out of the green leafy vegetables that you provide. These should still be given regularly to allow him an opportunity to choose. Undoubtedly, he cannot acquire a taste for new foods if they are not available.

A good gravel mixture should be provided in a separate dish. As an important source of minerals, gravel is wasted if used only on the cage bottom. A commercial gravel mixture is fine, but add a pinch of table salt whenever refilling the dish. Ask your pet dealer if he can get you "red cross grit" and crushed oyster shell. "Red cross" grit is usually of organic origin such as coral, barnacles, etc. Add these two ingredients to the commercial gravel as follows: to a two pound box of gravel, (which, hopefully, contains a bit of charcoal), add one pound red cross grit and one pound crushed oyster shell. This enriches the original mixture and is extremely important for breeding birds.

A cuttlebone or mineral block should always be present in the bird's cage.

Your bird will benefit from the following **vitamin and mineral supplements;** vitamins for the drinking water (Avitron by Lambert Kay is very good), oils for the seed, a few drops of cod liver or wheat germ oil (or Linatone by Lambert Kay) given three times a week, and Vionate, a powdered supplement to be sprinkled on fruits and vegetables. Your pet dealer will have these items for sale or can offer substitutes.

Once in a while you may want to treat your bird to some **millet spray**, an **egg biscuit**, or the seed toys made for budgies and parakeets.

Cockatiels need to chew on calcium blocks of some sort. These two birds are eating the "bone" of a cuttlefish.

On the facing page, the author shows that if you move slowly and deliberately you will not create a panic when your hand enters the cage to select a bird for training.

Fresh branches from trees and bushes, like oak, maple, citrus or other fruit trees, and hibiscus are nourishing. Be absolutely sure that these have not been sprayed with insecticide or other chemicals. Rinse branches well in fresh water before giving to your cockatiel.

If you are buying a **hand fed baby** there may be additional dietary requirements. Find out from the dealer what the youngster was reared on. How long has he been weaned? *Under no circumstances should you buy an unweaned baby!* Weaning is perhaps the most difficult part of successfully hand raising a cockatiel. Ask for the hatch date if available.

In the wild, cockatiels feed twice a day, in the morning and again in the afternoon. In captivity, most birds have food in front of them constantly. Owners feed their pets in the morning and leave the food all day. A newly acquired bird should have food available all day for at least two or three days, but as serious training commences you may want to initiate a **feeding schedule.** This is not to suggest that a bird be deprived of food, for no matter how training progresses a cockatiel should be fed every day.

Feeding schedules refer instead to **split rations**, morning or afternoon feedings, or double feedings. Split rations can help to train the bird to accept food from your hand, do tricks, even speak. Take the normal amount of feed that your bird consumes daily. Split it into three parts. Give one third before leaving for work in the morning. Use the next third during the training session when you get home. Give the rest, along with all remaining vegetables when you are finished training for the evening. Always give some leafy vegetable in the morning, as the birds seem to eat most of it early.

If you are at home all day, split the rations into more parts. Do some training in the early morning before you feed him in his cage. Give him some seed in a dish at midday. Use seed every time you deal with the bird. Always be sure to give him enough to eat in the cage and time to eat it when you are finished training for the day.

Double feedings refer to double rations, usually necessary for breeding birds, very young babies and those recovering from illness.

If your new bird won't eat, don't panic! Birds are usually upset by changes of environment and one or two days without eating isn't very serious. You may want to check with the pet shop to see what previous diet the bird was given. Above all, don't constantly bother the bird. Give him an opportunity to settle down and accept his new surroundings.

When a cockatiel that you have had for some time suddenly stops eating, there is cause for concern. Observe him for any other behavioral changes. Consult a veterinarian. He will probably ask you to bring the bird to his office for examination. If he feels that your bird is not ill he may recommend an appetite stimulant. Val Syrup and Nutrical are excellent. Never wait too long before speaking to the vet if your bird stops eating. Due to their fast metabolic rate, weight loss can be extremely quick and possibly fatal.

It is useful to **measure the normal daily intake** of your bird when he is in good health and eating well. Take a measuring cup. and find out how much feed his dishes hold when full. If you fill them only half way, measure that amount. When refilling the seed dish clean out the empty seed shells and measure the remaining amount. Subtract it from the total amount that you put in. This is his normal daily intake and is the amount that you should offer each day. Do not base the amount on your findings of just one or two days. Use one week or more to determine the bird's normal intake.

If your bird eats all that is offered, add a bit more the next day. A bird's appetite increases and decreases according to his physiological activities. **During moulting**, for instance, the process of feather replacement can increase the nutritional needs of the bird. In cold weather, the need to produce body heat can increase the appetite. Ideally, you should remain flexible and learn to adjust the bird's diet as needed.

If your bird eats a good amount but appears to **lose weight** definitely **see your veterinarian.** There are a number of possible causes but don't try to diagnose your bird's problem unless you are willing to gamble with his continued good health.

Cleaning the bird cage and accessories should be done routinely. Each day scrub the water dish with hot water and soap. Use a bottle brush or sponge to remove any residue. Scrub

The photographer moved to within a foot of this bird to photograph her. She didn't move away, indicating she was a good taming possibility. On the facing page, the author has just placed a white cockatiel on the training stand preparatory to advanced lessons.

the feed dishes at least twice weekly, more often if the bird defecates in or on them. Clean the cage bottom daily. Check the droppings, and the amount of feed, eaten and uneaten. For covering the bottom you can use newspaper or commerically prepared paper. In very large cages or outdoor aviaries, wood chips or sand might be more appropriate.

Perches should be cleaned with sand paper or a perch scraper to keep them free of food residues and feces. Never give your bird wet perches to stand on. Let them dry completely before replacing in the cage. **Wet perches** can lead to colds and arthritic conditions. Wash and dry the cage bottom once a week with hot water and soap. Clean and dry the bottom grill at the same time. Cage bars should be sponged off periodically with plain water to keep the cage shining and in tip-top shape.

Commercial bird sprays are fine to use on the cage, but use them sparingly on your indoor pet. **Oil base sprays** should not be used on any cockatiel. If you feel that your bird has **external parasites,** look for evidence. Horizontal marks running across the heavy wing and tail feathers usually indicate lice. Cover the cage with a white cloth at night to check for mites. They are usually attracted to the white cloth and will cling to it, showing up as very tiny little specks. It is unlikely that a cockatiel kept indoors would have a parasite infestation if you didn't bring him home with them, so don't automatically suspect "bugs" if your bird occasionally scratches. All birds scratch while preening. If their nose or head itches, they scratch, just like people. It is far easier to **prevent "bugs"** by keeping the cage clean and allowing your bird to bathe often in fresh water than to eradicate them once established.

Feather shine sprays should not be used on cockatiels.

Among the necessities for keeping cockatiels are: suitable cages, a vitamin-mineral supplement, fresh greens such as this branch torn from a kumquat tree and a liquid food supplement to balance the daily diet.

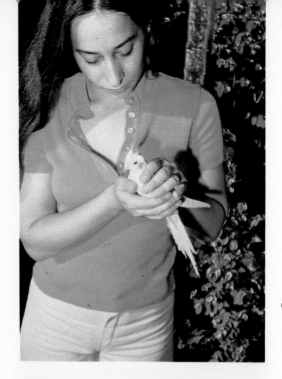

One of the real tests for a tame cockatiel is as follows: hold the tamed bird very lightly and gently in your cupped hands.

Gently raise your upper hand so the bird is resting on your bottom hand without feeling restrained from flying away.

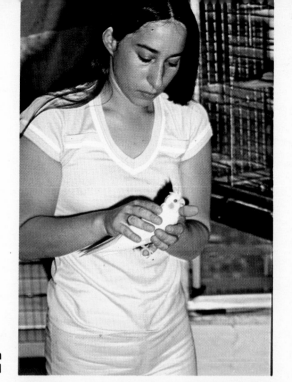

As soon as you feel him raise his body and prepare to fly away . . .

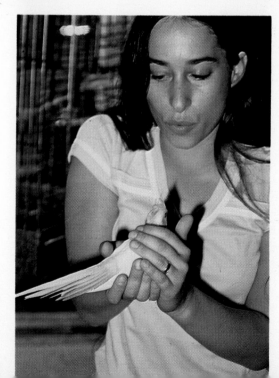

. . . you must quickly, but gently, replace your hand to restrain him from flying away.

A suitable cockatiel cage has strong wires, a large door and a bottom grill.

A cockatiel and his playground.

II
Equipment

THE WORLD'S LARGEST SELECTION OF PET, ANIMAL, AND MUSIC BOOKS.

T.F.H. Publications publishes more than 900 books covering many hobby aspects (dogs, cats, birds, fish, small animals, music, etc.). Whether you are a beginner or an advanced hobbyist you will find exactly what you're looking for among our complete listing of books. For a free catalog fill out the form on the other side of this page and mail it today.

. . CATS . . .

. . . BIRDS . .

. . . ANIMALS . . .

. . . DOGS . . .

. . FISH . . .

. . . MUSIC . . .

Before bringing the bird home, have all the **necessary equipment.** Feed, cage, extra cups and dishes, a cage cover, and training sticks and a stand if you plan to use one. Set up the cage with food and water and choose a location for it. Decide on the primary trainer, the person who will tame the bird. Think of a few possible **names** for your bird and choose the one that seems appropriate. If you are planning to do speech training a one or two syllable name is recommended (such as Leo, Cleo, Mike, Mary, etc.). Three and four syllable names may be too difficult for the bird to say.

Transport the bird from pet shop to home in a box with air holes cut in the sides. If you live in a cold climate be sure to keep the bird warm while transporting him. It is best not to take a bird out in the rain, even in a box, for this increases the chance that he

A typical cockatiel playground, available at most petshops.

A specially made cockatiel cage will have wires which run parallel to the floor so that the cockatiel can climb, and it will have seed cups (lower photograph) which are easily cleaned.

The ideal cockatiel cage has heavy parrot-wire construction and should have dimensions of about 26'' x 20'' x 20''. The cage should be 100% metal, preferably a stainless steel or non-rusting metal. The grill bottom should have an easily removable tray underneath to facilitate cleaning (see photo on facing page). Toys can be added at a later date. Swings of some type are useful, because many cockatiels like to roost on swings. Perches are a necessity. The best perch diameter for a cockatiel is ½'' to ¾''; dowels or natural wood can be used, and it is good to provide a variety of diameters.

It is advantageous to get the largest cage you can afford, for then it will be useful for a larger bird or for breeding purposes.

may catch cold. If possible, bring the bird home in the morning to give you the maximum amount of time to work with him the first day.

When **buying a cage,** look for standard heavy parrot wire, not light, thin budgie wire. Dimensions should be about 26 inches high, 20 inches wide and 20 inches deep. Get a metal cage in preference to a wooden or painted one. Metal cages last longer and are easier to maintain. Wooden cages won't hold cockatiels for very long, as they will chew right through them.

A **bottom grill** is advisable to keep the bird out of his own debris. Either wire or solid closed tops are fine. The door should be large enough to get your hand through with the bird on it without touching at any point. Birds are very nervous about moving through small doors on a hand.

Bells provide hours of entertainment. Just be sure that the clapper is secure inside the bell. **Mirrors** should not be given to the bird if you expect him to speak. **Ladders** can be purchased made of both plastic and wood. You may want to invest in an entire playground setup for your pet; ask your pet shop owner about it.

There is a big difference between taming and training.

Clipping one of your bird's wings can serve to make training easier than it might otherwise have been, **but it is very important to remember that a cockatiel still retains a good amount of flying ability even with a wing clipped.** Therefore it is not safe to assume that a wing-clipped cockatiel can be left alone and not fly into a dangerous situation.

III
Taming

Before bringing your new bird home, consider the **training area**. Use a small room like the bathroom or hallway. This area is best isolated from the rest of the house. Cover wall mirrors and any large windows into which the cockatiel might fly. Trying to tame a bird in a living room or den can be an exercise in futility. The bird usually ends up on the curtain rods or under the couch. If the floor is tile, cover it to cushion any falls.

Clipping one of your cockatiel's wings to facilitate taming is recommended. Taming can be achieved without clipping the wing, but the bird has considerably more mobility. Clipping is not permanent and once the bird is tame you can decide whether to reclip in the future (every 5-6 months) or let him fly. If you want to take the bird out in the yard you must clip him and keep a close watch on the growth of new flight feathers. An indoor pet that flies loose must be protected from open doors. Hand-fed cockatiels do not need their wings clipped for taming purposes.

If you have decided to clip the bird's wing, ask the pet shop to help you with it before you take him home unless you are experienced and plan to do it yourself. It is best not to grab and restrain the bird too often. In addition, by clipping the bird at the shop, you avoid connecting the bad experience with the new surroundings. Clip only one wing. By clipping both wings you give the bird too much control over the direction of his flight. He is more quickly discouraged from attempting to fly if his flight curves away from the chosen direction. Some people recommend that the wing feathers be plucked out instead of clipped. They reason that new feathers will grow in more quickly. This is true, but feather growth causes strain on the bird's system. The bird should be stressed as little as possible during the adjustment period, making clipping the preferred method.

Plan what you are going to do before beginning. You need good light, a pair of clippers (small wire cutters are perfect),

Leave the first two feathers, cut the next two feathers with scissors, then clip the next six feathers with the wire cutters.

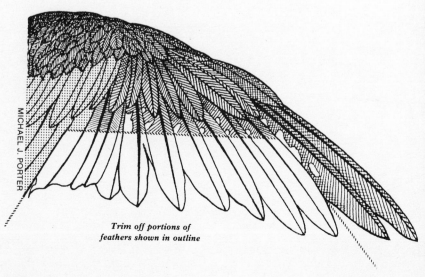

MICHAEL J. PORTER

*Trim off portions of
feathers shown in outline*

scissors and *"Quick Stop"* in case of bleeding. You must be able to recognize **blood feathers** from those that you can clip. Blood feathers are **new feathers** that are not finished growing in. They have blood vessels in the shaft to nourish the new feather as it grows and a direct line into the vascular system. Blood feathers must not be cut or clipped. Look at feather shafts carefully to make sure that you can identify any blood feathers that may be present.

Hold the wing firmly at the bend and extend it to give a clear view of the **primary and secondary flight** feathers. The four long feathers on the end of the wing are the primaries. Leave the first two feathers (1 & 2) as they are and cut the next two feathers (3 & 4) in half with the scissors. Now take the clippers and clip the next 8 to 10 feathers at the point where the feather emerges from the shaft. Leave at least ¾ inch of feather shaft emerging from the wing. Before beginning to clip, push the under-coverts back to fully expose the feather shafts. Look at each feather before you clip it to be absolutely certain that it isn't a blood feather. Try not to cut the over-coverts to preserve the appearance of the wing.

One very experienced person must **clip the wing** and another must **hold the bird**. The holder is responsible for watching the bird's respiration and holding the bird still. Use two hands to hold the bird. Put your thumb under the lower mandible, with the rest of your fingers around the head. Support the head and neck, keeping the neck straight. Don't pull the head or push it into the body. Don't let the body twist. Use your other hand to hold the bird's feet and torso.

Never hold a cockatiel by the tail; you'll end up with a handful of feathers! Support the bird's body on your lap or a towel-covered counter.

Occasionally you may want to **clip the bird's claws.** Natural wood perches help minimize the necessity, for they keep the claws nicely trimmed. It is best not to clip the claws on new arrivals unless they are overgrown or curled. Badly overgrown claws should be clipped cautiously to avoid cutting the vein. By making certain that you work in good light, you should be able to

Hold the cockatiel properly.

One person then isolates the foot.

The nail is then clipped off above the vein to prevent bleeding.

Then the nail is filed to eliminate rough edges which might catch in fabric.

see the vein through the claw. Have *"Quick Stop"* ready in case you hit the blood vessel. Styptic pencil is too hard.

Take the clippers and just tip each claw. You can always take more off. If you hit blood, take the claw and dip it in *"Quick Stop"* powder. You may have to pack it in with your fingertip. Be sure that the bleeding has stopped before you continue. Very tame birds will usually allow their owners to file their claws. This method is preferred to holding and clipping. File any rough edges from your cockies' claws so they don't catch in any material or your clothes. This could injure your cockatiel when he flies away.

Occasionally a **bird's beak** will become overgrown. With the right type and amount of chewing material this rarely happens. The overgrown beak must be trimmed to prevent it from interfering with normal eating. Consult your vet for help with this problem.

From the **first taming session** to any advanced training that you may attempt, you will find **food a helpful aid.** Offer the bird food to help win his confidence. During taming more seed will probably end up on the floor than in your bird's beak, but use it anyway. He must learn to accept food rewards from your hand if you plan to try further training.

Commercially available **millet sprays** seem to be the big favorite with cockatiels. Cut the sprays into three inch lengths for use during training sessions. Also offer sunflower seed. As you get to know your cockatiel better, you will discover which are his favorite foods. If possible, use these for rewards in advanced training.

*Never use a **leg chain** on a cockatiel!* Should he fight the chain, he could easily break his leg. You can accomplish the same goal (keeping the bird in one spot) by perch training and clipping the wing.

Toys will not be of much use in the initial taming sessions, but as your daily routine shapes up they may become very useful. Playing with the bird with a bit of rope, leather or a bell can help develop a good rapport between you. He will consider your rings, earrings, necklaces and other jewelry as his personal playthings, as you'll soon discover.

Watching your cockatiel **in front of the mirror** can be very amusing. The bird whistles to his image, struts around and shows his wings to the beautiful bird in the mirror. As mentioned earlier, however, mirrors distract the bird and should not be placed in his cage or near his stand.

HOW TO TAME THE COCKATIEL: THE FIRST HOUR

When you get the bird home, avoid commotion. The chosen trainer should stay with the bird, *all others go*. Take him into the pre-designated training area. It is best to handle the bird before transferring him to the new cage. You may be able to tame him in the first session. Many cockatiels have naturally good dispositions, making taming a simple task.

Use a soft tone of voice to reassure the bird. Move slowly to let him see what you are up to. *Never grab his body or pick him up from behind*. Let the bird come out of the box onto the floor. Be certain that the floor is well cushioned against falls. This is very important and can save you a great deal of trouble. Be kneeling down to greet the cockatiel as he ventures out of the box. Talk to him and offer your hand. If you want to use gloves, get the tight fitting cotton or leather type. Large bulky gloves will scare the bird.

Work with him low to the floor at first to avoid having him take long falls. You can offer either your finger or your whole hand, fingers together, horizontal to his body. Push gently against his legs and body, just above the feet. He may step right on, or he may try to fly or run away. When he settles down, kneel next to him and offer your hand again. Use your other hand to help block his **escape attempts**. It sometimes helps to work him from the corner of the room. The bird may hiss at you and try to bluff you by fluffing his feathers. Don't shy away if he tries these tactics or you'll never get past the first session.

If the **bird bites** he can't do too much damage. Do not hit the bird if he bites you. Tell him **"NO"** in a loud voice and remove your finger from his beak if it is still there. If he persists in biting take a piece of millet spray and put it right in his mouth as he tries to bite you. Keep working on getting him to step on your hand while you let him know that you're not afraid of his bite. This stage is critical. If the bird knows you're afraid, you are lost!

At this point it would be a good idea to remember your determination to tame your new cockatiel. **Be patient, move slowly and persist in your efforts.** When the bird steps on your hand, stay as still as you can. Don't try to move with the bird immediately. Let him sit still; he is probably panting to get rid of excess body heat. Birds do not have sweat glands. Excess body heat is expelled through the respiratory system.

Talk softly to the bird and keep repeating his name. Try to touch him with your other hand. Move very slowly so that the bird hardly notices. Touch his feet first and just let your finger rest there for a minute. Move it up slowly until you are touching the feathers on his stomach. Wait. Talk to the bird. Bring the bird close to your body and keep him facing you if possible, to block escape attempts. If you have to turn the bird around, gently touch his tail and he should turn.

Try to **touch and pet his chest** and chin; work your way up to the red ear coverts and his head. Once you can pet his head, you are just about done with the initial taming. Offer the bird some drinking water from his cup. He is probably hot and thirsty.

Try to have the bird step from one hand to the other. Give him a slow drill on stepping from hand to hand. Try again to pet the bird. **Be patient**, move slowly and try to keep the bird facing you.

At this point you can either put the bird in his cage and wait until later or place him on a low stand, let him rest a few minutes and continue. You have now reached the end of your first hour with the cockatiel; it is the most difficult.

THE FIRST DAY

The trainer should arrange to **spend the first day at home with the new cockatiel.** If other birds are present in the house, keep the bird out of their sight and sound as much as possible. Continue to tame the bird in short intensive lessons. Practice having him step from the stand to your hand. Work with the bird in the same training area as before. Keep his cage out of the training area. Encourage the bird to accept you and the stand as security objects, rather than the cage.

One of the most aggravating parts of training a bird is **getting**

46

it out of and into the cage. If he does not want to come out on your hand, see if he will come out by himself or on a stick.

As he begins to get used to the new surroundings, he will hop out of his cage whenever you open the door. Repeat the hand to hand training every time you take him out of the cage. Pet the bird as much as he will allow. Offer him millet. Talk to him and keep him with you as long as you want.

On the first day, try to accomplish **stick training.** Put the bird on the stand and approach him slowly with a short stick. Push against his legs gently to make him step up. Lift him off the stand and bring him over to you. Repeat this a few times. You may consider stick training an unneccessary task, but it comes in handy if the bird ever gets out of your reach, on the curtain rods or book shelves.

Continue these short lessons in a small area until you feel confident that you can walk into another room with the bird. You will learn to walk slowly and smoothly the longer you have a cockatiel riding on your hand or shoulder. When you are finished training for the day, put him in his cage. Give him his dinner and time to eat it before covering his cage for the night.

THE FIRST WEEK

The kind of routine that you develop with your bird in the first week is very important. If you work or go to school, feed and clean the bird in the morning. Take advantage of this time to talk to the bird and teach him his name. You should begin **training lessons** as soon as you get home to give maximum time to the bird each evening. Continue the regimen of the first day. Work on walking with the bird throughout the house. Let him perch on your shoulder if he so desires. Many cockatiels like to sit on your head.

Start training the bird to a **high stand** when you think he is ready. Use your judgment as to whether he will stay on the high stand or not. Choose a spot for the high stand in the room where you plan to spend the most time with your cockatiel. Like the cage, the stand must not be placed in a drafty or busy spot.

Introduce other family members to the cockatiel one at a time as soon as the bird has learned to step up on your hand. The other family members can practice hand training with the bird.

Very young children need supervision. When you are finished training for the night, put him in his cage, let him eat and cover his cage for the night.

THINGS TO REMEMBER

The more time you put into training the bird, the faster you'll get results. **Use short lessons** and deal with the bird often. Be patient, move slowly. Cover all mirrors present in the training area. Begin taming the bird in a different room than his cage is in. Use a small room; cover the floor to cushion any falls the bird may take.

One trainer should tame the bird initially. Taming consists of stick, hand, perch and pet training. Other members of the family should get to know the bird as soon as he is hand tame. Get the bird out of the cage and onto the stand as soon as possible.

When deciding on a trainer, choose a calm, patient person. The person who initiated the purchase of the bird or the one with the most time to devote to taming is the logical choice.

The daily routine should include feeding and cleaning. Scrub the water dish and supply fresh feed. Conduct the regular lessons, hand, stick and pet training. Give the bird free time on the stand (no lessons). Let him spend time with the family before putting him away for the night.

The Teitler Method of cockatiel taming and training: (1) One person tames the bird until it can be handled (2) without biting. The bird is then introduced to other members of the family (3) by hand-perching and using a stick as a perch (4). The cockatiel is then introduced to a free perch (5) and is trained to be lifted off the perch without flying away (6). Then he is trained to be comfortable when handled (7).

3

7

4

2

5

6

Birds bite because they are frightened.

You can look into a bird's face and see if it is frightened or secure. Only unfrightened birds are trainable.

IV
Special
Behavior
Problems

Biting is the most obvious behavior problem that you may encounter. Birds bite because they are frightened or nervous. Perhaps they are **older birds** that have been mishandled, or never handled at all. If the bird bites, try stick training before hand training. Never hit the bird or spray water on him. Use a loud **"NO"** if he goes to bite you. Use millet to distract him.

Sometimes your bird will **whistle** for long periods of time. Usually he is trying to get your attention. He wants to come out or he hears other birds outside. When you want to stop him from whistling, cover his cage. Remove the cover when he quiets down. Don't leave him covered when he is quiet.

Hissing is a normal response when the cockatiel is disturbed with the approach of strangers, if you peek under his cover once he is sleeping, or if you bother him while he's eating. This is a defensive posture for the bird and he is entitled to use it.

Cockatiels are avid **chewers.** To keep him from chewing your important papers, school work, books, music, curtains, wall paper and other household objects, perch train the bird to a stand. Give him plenty of chew toys to direct this normal activity. You will find that the cockatiel also chews up his own things. The paper that lines the bottom of his cage, his toys and possibly his feathers. This is rarely a problem with a well adjusted cockatiel. If you have provided a well balanced diet, plenty of free time out of the cage and enough chewing material you will probably never encounter a feather chewing cockatiel.

Don't house your cockatiel in a wooden-framed cage. The bird will chew through it in a short time and escape.

Your bird may turn out to be an **escape artist.** A clipped bird is not too difficult to catch. Find the bird, offer your hand or a stick if he is tame. A wild bird with a clipped wing will try to run from you. If you have a bird net, net him and return him to his cage, unless you plan to do some training. A light towel thrown over the bird in the absence of a net will accomplish the same thing.

A flying bird is obviously more difficult **to retrieve.** Dim the lights, but don't make the room too dark. Shut doors to restrict his flight. Use your hand or a stick with a tame cockatiel. With a wild bird, a net is your best resort. It is easier on the bird and you. A towel is the second choice.

52

The cockatiel will take advantage of doors with easy open latches to **escape**. Such doors must be repaired or given an additional latch. To prevent escape during initial taming sessions isolate the training area. Structure the situation to give you optimum control. Avoid confusion. Don't chase the bird excitedly.

If he should get out the door into the yard, retrieve as fast as possible with net, towel or gloves. If your bird flies into a tree, don't scare him out of the yard. Place his cage with food, water and millet spray in his clear view. If another cockatiel is available, place him in his cage next to the empty one as a draw. Wait. Hopefully, you will retrieve him successfully. Immediately take the bird indoors and clip him. If you prefer not to clip the wing, be more careful in the future.

After a period of time and many daily lessons you may decide that you have purchased **an untamable cockatiel**. Although this is highly unlikely, you may have a bird that is very nervous, or a biter. Cockatiels, like people, have many different personalities. Consider the problem carefully. If you have not adhered to the necessary training routine, there is no point in getting a different bird. If you have *really tried* to tame your cockatiel and failed, you may want to get another bird, a young one, and try again.

A good pet shop will trade in a bird which is untamable. Talk to the pet shop where you purchased the bird. Possibly, they will give you a partial credit toward another bird. Don't expect to be able to trade even for another cockatiel; that is unrealistic. At best you can get your old bird a good home where he will fit in. Be prepared to spend more money for a new bird.

One man birds are trained to be that way. The person that pays the most attention to the cockatiel is going to become his favorite person in the household. The same is usually true of your dog. He may allow the most intimate handling from that person and hold all others at bay. To avoid creating one man birds, have all family members share the task of feeding and cleaning. Attention is the key. Those who feed the bird from their hands, offering him little treats like millet spray, are going to become his friends. Game playing, as mentioned earlier, also helps to establish a good relationship with the bird.

A bird must be tame before it can be trained.

If you already have the bird stick-tame, you can retrieve him more easily if he flies to inaccessible places.

V
Training

There are definite differences between a **tame bird** and a **trained one.** Taming is the most basic form of training, consisting of stick, hand training and teaching the bird not to bite. A tame bird will not necessarily speak or let you pet him. This requires further training. A trained bird exhibits a greater variety of behaviors. These can be simple, but are usually complex behaviors that a tame bird has not learned.

How much and what kind of **advanced training** can you do with a cockatiel? Be realistic when you set goals for the bird. Speech training a cockatiel is realistic and worthwhile. Some birds develop a fairly extensive vocabulary. If you want a talking bird, try to purchase a male. Females can speak, but the male has more different natural sounds (listen to the songs he sings in the afternoon). Buy as young a bird as you can find.

There are many goals in training your cockatiel. Many people are content to have the bird perch on their knees (1) when called, or just to stay still while they have their heads scratched (2) or you might want your cockatiel to lie "dead" in your hand (3) or to fly onto your hand when you stick your hand into the cage (4). To assist in training, the wing feathers must be properly cut (5,6) so that the bird cannot fly out of your hand (7,8,9). A special perch with millet sprays attached is useful in training (10). When your cockatiels have been properly trained, you should be able to lift them out of their cage (11), cup them in your hand (12) and have them lie quiety for wing-clipping or nail-clipping (13).

When teaching the bird his first word, usually **"Hello"** or **"Hi,"** speak slowly and distinctly. Enunciate the word. Work on **"Hello,"** with the bird's name repeated after you say it. Work on only **one new word at a time.** The early morning and late afternoon, when birds sing their natural songs, is a good time to try **speech training.** You can give the bird his lesson inside or outside the cage. You can use a recording or teach him in person. If you want the bird to talk on command, you should teach him in person and reward him for every correct response. Recorded lessons can be made at home on cassettes of your own voice, or bought commercially. A woman or child makes the best speech trainer for a cockatiel. Their voices are closer to the natural pitch of the bird's voice. When speaking to your cockie, try to imitate this shrill voice.

Once your cockatiel has learned to say **"Hello"** you can go on to a short phrase such as **"How are you?"** Be sure to work on only one word or phrase at a time. The bird must be fairly fluent with one word or phrase before you begin teaching new material. Understand the difference between **responsive and imitative speech.** Responsive speech means that the bird will respond a certain way to a given cue. You say, **"What's your name?"** the bird replies, **"Leo"**. Imitative speech means that the bird will repeat what you say to him. You say, **"Hi,"** the bird replies, **"Hi."**

As mentioned earlier, you must keep the bird clipped if you plan to take him outside. **Don't leave the bird outside** by himself on a perch. (Think of cats!) When you first begin to take him into the yard, stay a good distance from any tall trees. Be sure that none of the neighborhood pets will jump at your bird and scare him off of his perch. Begin by taking the bird outside when it is quiet; place him on his stand. Stay near and watch how he adjusts to the new surroundings. Make the first visits outside fairly short. When you have trained him sufficiently to **stay outside** for longer periods, never leave your cockatiel in direct sunlight. Give him shelter from the breeze. On very warm days (over 72°) it is fine to give your bird a spray bath outside.

Training your cockatiel to **sit on a stand** may be some of the most valuable training that you do. Place the bird on the stand. If he jumps off, get him with your hand or a stick and put him back on. Repeat this as often as needed until he gets the idea. Reward the bird when he sits well. By outfitting the stand with some toys, you can make it more attractive to the bird.

Trick training a cockatiel requires that you understand the basics of a reward system. Reward the bird for desired behaviors; ignore, don't punish, undesired behaviors. Use food and praise to reinforce your bird's successful response. Reward for each repetition of the desired behavior.

Be realistic when deciding on a trick to teach. Cockatiels can learn to climb ropes and ladders. They can retrieve seed from a hanging cup, or place objects in a container. Train the bird to ring a bell for a seed reward. Don't expect to teach your cockatiel to ride bicycles or roller skate. This is unrealistic. But if you graduate to a larger parrot, Ah. . . . .!

Give your bird **short lessons,** three to five minutes, as often as you like, but don't tire him. Teach only one trick at a time. End your lesson before your bird stops attending to it. Try to end on a high point; praise and reward the bird.

The best way to decide on a trick to teach is by capitalizing on your bird's natural antics. He might display his wings and tail feathers. Train him to do it on command. See if he will roll over in your hand. Unusual for a cockatiel, but possible! As you get to know your bird, watch for **individualized behaviors.** Use these to shape a training schedule for your cockatiel.

Once you begin training, be certain to **repeat the lessons** every day. Trick training the bird on weekends, or twice a week, is a waste of time and frustrating for both you and the bird.

If your bird sits quietly on a perch, all puffed up, it has a health problem.

Hold the bird upside down and examine his vent (it must be dry) and feel his chest (it must feel full).

VI
First Aid

One of the first lessons that *you* must learn as a bird owner is that **accidents can happen.** They can happen in the taming process. A bird that has the freedom of the house can have run-ins with other family pets, large picture windows, or mirrors. You could come home to find your pet cockatiel twisted in a toy that you once thought was safe.

First of all, DON'T PANIC. A smart bird owner should acquaint himself with useful first aid preparations. By all means seek the advice of a veterinarian for follow up care, but in some situations you must act quickly.

Use **hydrogen peroxide** available at the drug store to stop bleeding and as an antiseptic to clean wounds. Get some *"Quick Stop"* from a farm supply or ask your pet shop to get it for you. *"Quick Stop"* is especially useful to stop bleeding when clipping

While it is acceptable to keep your cockatiels with other birds (such as these plum-headed parakeets) observe that the birds don't bully each other. It also would be very foolhardy to place a sick bird close to any other bird. Isolate any bird which you suspect of being ill.

claws, or if your bird should break a blood feather. Buy a commercial bird salve to dress cuts. **Vaseline** is a good salve, but be sure not to spread it all over the bird. It takes a long time to wear off the feathers. Also available at the pharmacy is B.F.I. antiseptic powder. Used to sprinkle on open cuts, it also helps to stop bleeding. Buy these medications and keep them on hand in the medicine chest. Have a **veterinarian's phone number** in your telephone book so that you won't have to search for it in an emergency. *Act first, then call the vet!*

If your bird cuts himself, clean the wound off with hydrogen peroxide. **Stop the bleeding** by holding a cotton swab with peroxide against the wound. Sprinkle with B.F.I. powder or use a bird salve to dress the wound. *Never cover the cut* with tape or bandage. This will only irritate the bird and he will pull it off anyway.

If you suspect that your cockatiel has **broken a leg or wing,** keep the bird quiet and warm. Remove all high perches from the cage. Put food and water within easy reach. Restrict the bird's activity and speak to your vet. Avoid moving a bird having any suspected broken bones. As with wounds, binding the area does little good.

A bird with a **broken leg** is smart enough to favor the leg while it heals. Most birds mend well if given a good diet and left undisturbed during convalescence. **Broken wings** usually droop down on the body or angle up unnaturally. Don't try to set the wing. Let it hang loose and talk to the vet. He will probably recommend leaving it the way it is, unless the break is extremely severe, twisting the wing out in a bad position. Again, the bird will favor the injury while it heals. Restrict the bird's activity and give plenty of food, vitamin and mineral supplements, and fresh green leafy vegetables.

Broken or clipped claws that bleed should be dipped in *"Quick Stop"* powder. Use hydrogen peroxide if you don't have *"Quick Stop."* Put the bird in his cage and leave him alone. If the bleeding continues at a fast rate you may have to grab him again and pack the bleeding claw with the powder. Put him down as soon as possible, for a struggling bird's heart beats faster than one sitting quietly in a cage.

Treat a **broken blood feather** the same way, with *"Quick Stop."* Sometimes a broken blood feather must be pulled because every time the bird flaps his wings it bleeds. Seek the help of an experienced person or a vet to pull out blood feathers, *unless you have done it or been shown how to do it.* Refrain from looking at the bird constantly to allow him to rest while the blood congeals.

Suspect illness if your daily check on the **bird's droppings** reveals bright green, brown or loose, watery droppings. Not just one or two bad droppings, but a whole day's worth. Watch for any sudden decrease in **appetite**. A bird that sits **fluffed up**, sleeping all day should visit the vet for an examination.

Birds with **colds** have the same symptoms as people with colds. They sneeze, not once or twice while preening the feathers, but often, possibly accompanied by **nasal discharge.** The eyes may become red and inflamed. The bird may **cough and wheeze.** After a complete examination, your vet will probably prescribe an antibiotic and possibly an ophthalmic ointment for sore eyes.

The most often recommended antibiotics are tetracycline and its derivatives, and chloromycetin. Never give your bird an antibiotic drug *prescribed* for people. Although the drug might have the same name, the dosage for a person could easily kill your cockatiel. Always let your vet prescribe the kind and dosage of any medication given to the bird.

You must keep the bird very warm when he is ill. 90°-95° is about right. Cover the cage and use a strong, light heater to radiate heat. Monitor the temperature with a thermometer. Most cockatiels are strong enough to throw off a simple cold, but if you fail to detect and treat it, the simple cold can become much more serious. Respiratory conditions such as **asthma, pneumonia, aspergillosis** and **chronic sinus** infections usually begin as colds. These conditions are difficult to treat and are often fatal.

It is best to prevent serious illness by scrubbing the water cup, cleaning the cage bottom, and checking the droppings daily. Also, provide fresh feed, fruit and vegetables, as well as the necessary vitamin and mineral supplements. House the bird out of drafts and don't keep him up all night to entertain your friends.

Psittacosis, a respiratory disease, is extremely rare in caged house pets. Caused by viral agents, the symptoms resemble atypical pneumonia. Psittacosis may occur when birds are housed in crowded, dirty cages and fed an inadequate diet with foul water. This is rarely the case with a house pet. All birds imported into the United States must be quarantined for psittacosis and other diseases, assuring that the birds passed through are free of the disease. For this reason, you should never buy a bird that may have been smuggled into the country. The price might seem right until you discover illness in your new pet. Buy all birds from reputable pet dealers and breeders. If your pet cockatiel develops a severe cold, do not suspect psittacosis. Take the bird to the vet as soon as illness is noticed.

Sinus trouble is indicated by swollen, red eyes and a discharge from the nostrils. If left untreated, the bird could develop a sinus knot on his forehead, and the condition may continue to worsen. Your vet will probably prescribe the same antibiotic medications that he uses to treat colds. Again, keep the cockatiel warm and quiet.

Whenever your bird is ill, offer him as much to eat as he wants. If he gets picky, offer him his favorite foods and let him eat as much as he can. Although a balanced diet is important when your bird is sick, it is more important that he eats plenty.

Digestive disorders may accompany colds or appear by themselves. **Constipation** is indicated by droppings devoid of green fecal matter. All the droppings show as white and clear matter. **Diarrhea** is more prevalent than constipation. Usually diarrhea is a symptom of some other illness. Sometimes a bird will stop passing waste material completely. This is extremely serious, for without treatment the bird's entire system will be poisoned rapidly. When you suspect any digestive disorder, go over the diet that you have been giving and seek advice from a qualified vet.

Going light refers to weight loss and usually indicates some other disorder. Try to rule out worm infestation as the cause of weight loss by providing the vet with a fresh stool sample to examine. Adjust the diet to provide more fattening foods like oats and more sunflower than parakeet seed. Offer milk-soaked wheat bread as well as corn kernels. The bird's dietary requirements may be changing. Ask your vet for an appetite stimulant if you think it necessary.

Feather problems rarely occur with a happy, well fed cockatiel. An unusually heavy, constant moult is a definite feather problem. Check the diet, and make sure that you are not artificially overheating your bird. Sometimes **birds chew their feathers.** This may be as a result of a poor diet or a high level of anxiety.

Ingrown feathers appear as lumps that begin at the base of the feather follicles and grow larger as the feather grows and tries to push out. Ingrown feathers must be treated by experienced people or your vet. Occasionally, a **double feather** grows on the wing or tail. There is no cause for concern unless the double feather bleeds. Usually the double feather grows out properly and eventually drops out in a moult. It may or may not grow back the same way.

Tumors, lumps and **bumps** can occur anywhere on the bird's body. They can be on the skin or internal. If you suspect a tumor, take the bird to the vet. It may be fatal, but usually is not. The vet may choose to remove the tumor. Many tumors grow to

1

2

These four photographs show the steps in training your bird to stay in your hand. First, hold the bird gently but firmly (1). If he wriggles, hold him against your body (2) until he quiets down. Then extend your hands away from your body (3) and slowly release your grip (4).

4

3

You should be able to hold your trained cockatiel in your palm without the bird biting you or trying to escape. This is the least you should expect from your cockatiel training.

a certain size and do not seem to affect the bird's general health for years. Sinus knots are often mistaken for tumors by inexperienced bird owners.

Foot problems and **lameness** can occur in both young and old birds. Arthritis and rheumatism can be caused by making the bird sit on wet perches, or perches too small to give him a proper grip. Arthritic birds must be kept warm and given perches of differing shapes and diameters. Make sure the diet is well balanced and supplemented.

If your bird appears to be lame or have a sore foot it may help to soak the affected area in warm water for five minutes. Better yet, hold the bird's bad leg under warm running water. Use a light stream of water, not too warm, and try not to get the bird wet all over. When five minutes have passed, dry the leg gently and paint with iodine or mercurochrome. Don't cover the area with any sort of bandage. Call your vet and tell him the symptoms and how you have treated them. He may suggest a different sort of first aid. Again, check the content of the bird's diet. Green leafy vegetables and vitamin and mineral supplements are very important if your bird comes up lame.

Occasionally, a bird develops **paralysis.** This may be due to a nervous system disorder. Keep the bird warm and place food and water within easy reach. See your vet as soon as possible.

Shock is a very serious condition that can occur as a result of injury. The bird stops moving and may make plaintive crying sounds or be silent. The eyes fail to focus and breathing becomes shallow. Immediately place the bird in a warm, protected spot. You may want to wrap him in a small towel or wash cloth. Don't continually fuss with the bird. He needs warmth, quiet, and rest. Put food and water within reach, although it may be some time before he tries to eat or drink. If the condition is a result of injury, apply first aid before placing the bird in his cage or, if you think it warmer, a small box. Warmth is imperative for a bird in shock.

Concussion resembles shock symptomatically. Usually the result of the bird flying head first into windows, walls, or mirrors, first aid treatment is the same as for shock. Try to prevent this by providing your flying cockatiel with a safe place in which to fly. Avoid large windows and mirrors in the flying space. Concussion can be fatal, so it is better to protect your bird than to treat the condition.

Egg binding can occur in single and breeding birds. Poor diet and insufficient exercise can cause the condition. Treatment can take various forms. Keep the bird very warm and quiet. If your cockatiel is tame, apply two or three drops of mineral oil to the vent. Don't try to push the egg out unless you have had previous experience, for it is fatal if the egg breaks inside the bird. Speak to your vet and ask his advice.

Some female cockatiels, like chickens, lay eggs on a regular schedule even in the absence of a mate. Give the bird plenty of flying time and a diet rich in minerals. Egg production causes a strain on the system and if mineral content in the diet is insufficient, the bird will draw on her own body calcium to make eggs. A well fed bird that gets plenty of exercise can pass eggs regularly with no harm. Try to distract the bird by giving her more attention. Above all, be certain that the diet is well-balanced and the bird is not becoming weak from the strain of egg laying.

RESUME

Remember, **a sick bird is best left in a warm, quiet cage**. Don't drag your bird to the vet for every little sneeze. Call and consult him for advice before you show up at his office. He will tell you if he wants to see the bird. It is far better to prevent illness by keeping the bird's cage clean and his diet balanced. Treatment is much more difficult and time consuming than preventive maintenance. Never administer drugs to your cockatiel without first consulting your vet. Don't wait long to consult the vet if your bird is losing weight or shows definite cold symptoms. Before you get to the vet, keep the bird very warm (90 to 95 degrees is about right) and quiet. When transporting him, try to avoid sudden temperature changes. To repeat, **a clean cage and good diet are the most important elements in preserving your bird's continued well-being**.

One of the main advantages of buying your cockatiel from a pet shop or bird store is the availability of reliable, experienced advice, as well as emergency equipment.

A **hospital cage** is usually available for rent or purchase from a pet shop that handles a lot of birds. This is a small cage which

When Risa Teitler started taming and training this bird, it bit her ferociously every time she gave it the chance. Within 15 minutes, however, the bird was perfectly tame and didn't bite any more.

It is not safe to let a pet cockatiel, even one that has had its flying ability restricted by wing-clipping, have complete freedom in outdoor surroundings, so don't let your birds fly free on your property. Remember that even a wing-clipped bird has enough mobility to escape—and remember also that even if it were impossible for it to escape it still would be subject to danger from predatory birds and other animals.

Vents

Door

Thermometer

Perch

Glass

Lamp

Hinges

Switch

Frame, linen top, perforated zinc underside.

A typical hospital cage. While you may consider renting one from a petshop, you would be well-advised to buy your own.

has a built-in heat source. It is mostly closed in to prevent drafts and to cut down the amount of light entering from outside the cage so as not to get the sick cockatiel excited. Ask your pet shop about the availability of a hospital cage the next time you visit him for seed, so you will know what is available to you.

If you have **more than one bird** you might consider buying your own quarantine cage. You'll want to use it for isolation and observation of newly acquired cockatiels (or any other bird for that matter) and for restraining and treating injured cockatiels.

This young lady has a dozen trained cockatiels. Cockatiels make excellent pets and great gifts to people who have the time to tame and train them. A self-supporting hobby is to train and tame cockatiels for your local petshop.

Stick training is a natural for cockatiels. By using a training stick (facing page), your cockatiel feels more secure. The stick can also be used to retrieve the bird if it flies into an inaccessible place. Holding the bird (above) should be part of the daily training regimen. The bird must always feel safe and secure when you hold him. This ensures that you will be able to clip the bird's nails and examine its feathers whenever you see fit.

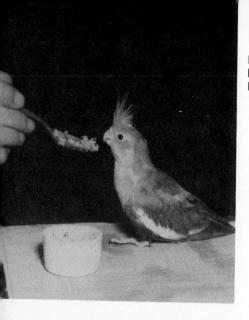

Hand-feeding your baby cockatiel is a last resort.

Budgies are naked when they hatch, unlike cockatiels, which are covered with down.

VII
Breeding

People who enjoy their cockatiels as pets often consider attempting to **breed** them. First, be aware that breeding birds are not usually tame to their owners once they begin rearing a family. Often, the most affectionate pets turn into aggressive, possessive parents. If possible, keep a single pet and buy other cockatiels for breeding.

Never breed related birds. Although some people feel that related pairs produce good offspring, it is genetic fact that flaws can be compounded and passed on. Young birds may attempt to nest and breed, but two year old birds are more reliable.

Try to determine if you are getting mature birds in good physical condition.

About four days old (above), this baby cockatiel shows a crop full of seed. (Photograph by Dr. Gerald Allen in Australia.) The advantage of hand-feeding a bird is that it becomes very tame, since it knows the person who feeds it as its "mother." Hand-fed babies, though usually weaker and less desirable than normally bred birds, are more easily trained, too. As soon as they come out of the nestbox you should place them on a perch so their training can start immediately.

Breeding cockatiels should be accustomed to a **well-balanced diet** *before you get them.* Otherwise you should delay their nesting until they have been on a proper diet for five to six months. This is to ensure that your hen will not become egg bound from poor nutrition. The parents may not feed the babies sufficiently if they have not been eating well prior to nesting. Nesting, egg laying, and rearing young stress the breeding bird's system. Poor nutrition could cause illness in the breeding pair, infertile eggs and deserted or sickly offspring.

The **breeding cage** must be large enough to allow the birds to fly across lengthwise. Good dimensions are four feet high, four feet long, two to three feet wide. The cage should be placed in a quiet location. Too much interference can discourage the birds from breeding. The breeding box should be placed in the cage so that you can observe the progress of the babies once they hatch.

Don't constantly bother the birds, but after you begin to hear sounds from the nest, you should check once a day to be sure that inexperienced parents are properly feeding the young. If not, you may have to **hand feed** to keep the babies alive. Try to avoid handfeeding. Parent-raised babies develop faster, grow larger and seem to be a bit hardier than hand-reared young.

Nest boxes can be made out of wood or cardboard. Wood lasts longer, but there is some advantage to being able to dispose of used boxes after each season. At the beginning of the next season you can replace with new boxes of the same kind. Good dimensions are twelve inches high, sixteen inches long and twelve inches wide. Cut the door in the lower left hand corner of the box, three inches from the bottom. The door should be big enough to allow the birds to pass through easily, but small enough to give them privacy inside the box. They will make adjustments to your design by chewing in their own architectural ideas.

Also, cut some **ventilation holes** on three sides of the box. The top of the nest box should open half-way to give you access to the inside. Should you need to take the babies, such access is imperative.

Cover the bottom of the box with wood shavings. Use pine bedding, but don't use cedar. Some birds will nest in cedar but pine shavings are preferred. Attach a nest frame to the rear right hand side of the box. Use one inch by one inch or two inch by two inch wood to make a nest frame. This will keep the eggs from rolling around in the box and getting chilled. The frame also keeps the babies close to one another, under the sitting parent. This helps keep the babies' temperature constant and high.

Use the same dimensions and design for a **wooden nest box**. Put hinges in the top to give you access to the inside of the box. At the start of each season, thoroughly clean and bug-spray the box. Allow twenty four hours after spraying before introducing the box to the birds. Put wood shavings in the bottom to a depth of two and one half inches. Be certain that your ventilation holes are adequate. Wood boxes are warmer than cardboard. Clean out the inside of the box once a week after the babies hatch, unless the parents are too disturbed. Don't change all the shavings, just try to remove any fungus or mold that may be growing on the droppings of the young birds. If the parents react too badly to the cleaning by biting you and trampling on the babies, don't persist. *You* could cause more harm than the *fungus!*

Most cockatiels like to **breed** in the autumn. Summertime in the hot climates is too hot for breeding your birds. Indoor breeding with temperature artificially controlled can be accomplished year 'round. **Before the breeding season** arrives, begin giving the potential parents an enriched diet. Replace the bird's **gravel** with a fresh mixture. Check every week to see if more gravel is needed. **Mineral block** or **cuttlebone** must be supplied. Fresh branches should be given often. Offer much more soft food (include corn kernels, peas, green leafy vegetables and bread). **Bread** can be made by toasting whole wheat bread and crumbling it into a dish. Add sunflower or millet meal and cod liver oil to the crumbled bread. Mix these ingredients together, adding some warm water to make it soft and crumbly. Don't add too much water or the mixture will become mushy and the birds won't eat it. Some cockatiels refuse to eat bread, but try to offer it anyway.

By all means give them the vegetables and fruits that they will accept, but continue to provide bread on a daily basis. *Don't let*

The proper way to hold a cockatiel (or any other parrot for that matter) is shown above. Your thumb goes under the lower mandible (beak) while your other fingers cradle the head. Your other hand holds the rest of the body down, including the feet. If you want to examine the wings (facing page), you need help. The person holding out the wing should do so carefully, using his thumb at the joint of the wing and then extending the feathers. This position is used for wing-clipping or for general inspection (looking for parasites).

1

2

(1) **A typical** cockatiel nest box (top removed) showing a clutch of five eggs. (2) A small cage with a nest box attached. (3) Three cockatiel eggs compared to a small chicken's egg. (4) Newly hatched chicks. (5) Cockatiel chicks about one week old.

Trim off portions of feathers shown in outline

To clip your cockatiel's wing feathers, follow the diagram, cutting about ten feathers of the wing, but leaving the two at the end of the wing uncut.

the bread sit overnight. Prepare fresh bread each morning for feeding parents.

Be certain that the vitamin regimen is complete. Administer these daily instead of two to three times a week.

The breeding birds must be able to fly within the breeding cage. **Exercise** is imperative for breeding birds. Consider exercise as important as a good diet. Lack of exercise is another cause of egg binding, infertile eggs, and added stress during breeding.

When you want to begin the **breeding season,** place the nest box inside the birds' cage. Go away and leave the birds alone to investigate. Every day feed and clean the birds and give them complete privacy the rest of the time. Be patient. Once they begin to customize the nest box and the hen begins to consume a great deal of gravel and mineral block it is just a matter of time before the first eggs arrive.

It may take four to six weeks for the birds to get started, but usually the pair gets to work immediately. Expect three to five eggs to a clutch. The eggs will be layed every other day and take eighteen to twenty one days to hatch. An indication that the hen has layed will show in the inordinate amount of droppings deposited on the bottom the cage. The birds take turns sitting on the eggs. Usually the hen sits from dusk to dawn and the cock from dawn to late afternoon, when the two of them spend some time together before the hen goes in for the night. Many pairs sit together on the eggs and the babies.

When the babies begin hatching you will hear sounds from the nest. Soft peeping from the babies as the parents feed them is a good indication of a successful hatching. The parents feed tiny amounts of food at first, but soon begin stuffing the babies until the crop appears to be distended. A well fed baby cockatiel looks overfed to the inexperienced eye. If the crop is stuffed with hard seed, the babies will not develop rapidly and may not derive the necessary nutrition from the parents' **regurgitated food.** If you see hard seed in the crop, be sure to offer green leafy vegetables liberally and plenty of soft bread.

The babies grow rapidly when fed properly and may be poking their heads out of the nest at four weeks of age. Pin feathers appear at about seven days to cover a nearly naked body. The heavy wing, tail, and crest feathers appear first. Then pin feathers begin to cover the crop, back and abdomen.

The first time that you see the **babies outside of the nest** is a thrill. The babies feel the same way and usually run back to the security of the box as soon as they see you. In a couple of days they get used to you and begin flapping their wings on the outside of the box. Prior to leaving the nest box, the babies practice flapping on the inside, making lots of noise that you will soon learn to recognize as **baby exercise.**

Babies leave the box for good at five to six weeks of age. They are still fed by the parents, but weaning begins immediately. The parents by then may already have more eggs in the nest. By eight weeks of age, most babies are eating independenttly and can be separated from the parents. Some cockatiels take longer to **wean** than others, especially if the parents are inexperienced. Be sure that the babies are eating on their own when you separate them from the parents or they may lose weight and become ill. At ten weeks the babies can usually go to new homes to be tamed for family pets. Ten week old cockatiels are not old enough to travel to the pet shop for resale.

Interrupt the breeding season after two clutches by removing the nest box.

Deserted or **abused** offspring may have to be hand-reared. By all means, encourage the parents to raise the young, but if this is not possible, set up an incubator and stabilize the temperature at 95 degrees before placing the babies in it. Handle the baby cockatiel as little as possible, take him out for feeding and replace him in the incubator before he gets chilled. A baby with no feathers cannot maintain his body heat for long. Wrap him in a towel and feed according to the following schedule. A one to four day old baby every two to three hours round the clock. A five to nine day old every four hours. At ten to fourteen days you can stretch the feedings to six hours. Continue at six hour intervals for the remainder of hand feeding. Fill the crop up and try to keep air out. You can gently push out excess air, but don't squeeze the chick. Feed with a very small spoon. It is almost impossible to overfeed. Offer the following diet: Use the bread mixture described earlier, warmed and softened with water. Add

1

2

A good breeding setup (1) where large
wooden nest boxes are made available to
the breeding cockatiels. (2) Young
cockatiels are quite a responsibility if you
want to hand-feed them. A spoon is probably easier to use than an eyedropper.

(1) A baby cockatiel about two weeks old. You must be certain that you have a pair of cockatiels if you want to breed them. The male (3) has a much brighter face than the female (2).

3 2

more sunflower meal than you would for the parents, but remember that it is concentrated. Add some prepared baby peas or green beans to replace the green leafy vegetables. Add a few drops of *Avitron*. Almost any formula that is well balanced and soft enough for the baby to take easily will be useful for hand-rearing.

Begin **weaning** the babies at seven to eight weeks of age. **Hand-reared** young usually remain dependent longer than parent-raised. Feed the babies in the morning and place sunflower, parakeet seed, millet spray, water and a portion of their formula in a dish on the bottom of the nursery cage. You will have to switch from the incubator to the nursery cage when the babies begin to fly. In the late afternoon, before covering the babies for the night, give them a good feeding by hand. Never put the babies to sleep without feeding them their fill.

Continue to wean the babies in this manner and soon you will see cracked seeds on the cage bottom. At this point offer green leafy vegetables in addition to the other feed and formula. By ten weeks you should be able to let the babies eat on their own all day and feed them just one time a day, in the afternoon. Watch the babies' progress. Baby cockatiels progress at their own individual rate. Adjust the schedule to fit the needs of the situation, but never skip feedings because it is inconvenient for you. If that is the case, better not try hand-feeding. Give the babies to someone who can raise them if *you* don't have the time.

Breeding cockatiels can be enjoyable or heartbreaking. Be certain that you will accept the confinement that breeding birds often means. If you are accustomed to an active social life, it is best to stick with a single pet, or you may find yourself in the uncomfortable position of deciding whether to let a baby bird live or die. Often, the breeding is unsuccessful. If you cannot take disappointment or if you are impatient, don't try breeding.

BIBLIOGRAPHY

The following books are available from your pet shop, bookseller or library. If you are at all serious about keeping cockatiels, you should scan through these books to get other points of view and to achieve a greater depth of understanding.

H-964 BIRD DISEASES, by Drs. Leslie Arnall and Ian Keymer. Ten years in preparation, this brilliant book represents the most complete and up-to-date book on the treatment of diseases of birds ever published. 528 pages in a 6 x 9" hard-bound format, it is heavily illustrated with almost 100 color photos and hundreds of magnificent detailed monochrome photos and line drawings, including some of the most graphically revealing and useful depictions of avian pathological conditions ever published. The immensely authoritative but easy-to-read text is systematically arranged for maximum reader benefit. A bonus appendix section includes a group of tables and charts that form an excellent permanent handy-reference guide. Bird owners—fanciers and dealers alike—*need* this book.
Retail

COCKATIEL HANDBOOK, By Gerald R. Allen and Connie Allen. ISBN 0-87666-956-9. TFH PS-741.
Contents: Introduction. Nymphicus Hollandicus And The Science of Taxonomy. Cockatiel Anatomy. Natural History of Cockatiels. Cockatiels As Pets. The Cockatiel Anatomy. Breeding Cockatiels. Diseases And Illnesses. Further Reading On Cockatiels And Parrots In General.
Audience: This authoritative new handbook on keeping and breeding cockatiels is the outgrowth of the many years of study and observation by a husband/wife team living in Australia. It contains practical up-to-date information and many colorful photos of cockatiels and other parrot-type birds.
Hard cover; 5½ x 8"; 256 pp. 96 black and white photos; 77 color photos.

THE ENCYCLOPEDIA OF COCKATIELS by George A. Smith. ISBN 0-87666-958-5. TFH PS-743. Contents: What Is A Cockatiel? The Cockatiel As A Pet Parrot. The Wild Cockatiel. Breeding Cockatiels. Problems In Breeding. A Guide To The Color Forms. Cockatiel Genetics. Diseases.
Audience: This excellent book is designed to help *all* cockatiel owners, beginners and experienced aviculturists alike. It covers every important aspect of cockatiel maintenance, feeding, housing, breeding and disease control and treatment and has a very fine section on cockatiel genetics and selecting breeders.
Hard cover; 5½ x 8; 256 pp. Heavily illustrated with both black and white and color photos.

White or lutino cockatiel.
Photo courtesy of the San Diego Zoo